MW01290021

THIS NOTEBOOK BELONGS TO :

Made in United States
Orlando, FL
27 January 2023

29102518R00055